Stealing The Midnight From a Handful of Days

Michele McDannold

PUNK HOSTAGE PRESS

Stealing The Midnight From A Handful Of Days
Michele McDannold

© Michele McDannold 2014

ISBN-10: 1940213010
ISBN-13: 978-1-940213-01-9

All rights reserved. Printed in the United States of America. No part of this text may be used or reproduced in any manner whatsoever without written permission from the author or publisher except in the case of brief quotations embodied in critical articles and reviews. For information address Punk Hostage Press, Los Angeles, California.

Punk Hostage Press
P.O. Box 1869
Hollywood CA, 90078
www.punkhostagepress.com

Editor: Iris Berry

Introduction: Bill Gainer

Cover Design: James Griffin

Cover Photo: Kari Spencer

Some of the poems were previously published in *Zygote in my Coffee, Red Fez Publications, Gutter Eloquence, Primal Urge Magazine, Ppigpenn, Meth Lab, Finger Magazine, Rattlesnake Review, Heroin Love Songs, Clutching at Straws, Kleft Jaw, Guerilla Pamphlets, Opium Poetry, Ebullience Press, Remark poetry, Juice Poetry, Poet Plant Press, The Musophobist, The Indite Circle, Medusa's Kitchen, Outsider Writers, Calliope Nerve, Luciferous, Modus Operandi Zine, Cherry Bleeds and Rusty Truck*

EDITORS ACKNOWLEDGMENTS

In July of 2012 Punk Hostage Press was invited to participate in the very first annual *Beast Crawl Collective* in Oakland California. It was an incredible experience where I met so many talented writers and poets. One of which was Michele McDannold. Both A. Razor and I felt an instant connection with Michele. And since that time Michele has been a part of the Punk Hostage Press family, the very bedrock on which she and I have formed an indelible friendship. A friendship that allowed me the distinct privilege of witnessing Michele evolve into an incredible woman who has been able to find her voice as a powerful poet and writer.

That being said, it is with great affection to have had the honor of working with Michele McDannold on her first book *Stealing The Midnight From a Handful of Days*. I want to Thank Michele for trusting me with her words and being so lovely to work with, it has been an absolute joy and I can honestly say that I am sad to see it end. A lot of laughing. And a lot of crying, the good kind, because the words insisted.

I would Also like to thank my partner and Co-Founder of Punk Hostage Press, A. Razor, who is a constant inspiration and without him this book would not be possible.

A huge and loving *Thank You* goes out to Bill Gainer for writing such a wonderful and heartfelt Introduction to this book. And, for his constant support and love for Punk Hostage Press, always.

To Kari Spencer for the cover photo and James Griffin for his cover design work. Their collaboration together made for a beautiful and haunting imagery resulting in a book cover befitting of it's incredible title and contents.

In Michele's own words:

"I would like to thank my Mom, my crazy but amazing kids, my bro Eric and all the other family that humor me occasionally. Punk Hostage Press! Iris Berry and A. Razor, Bill Gainer, Kari Spencer, Nick Boydstun, James Griffin, Shalonda Blan, Handyman Jason, Crazy Joe, Leopold McGinnis, Brian W. Fugett, Michael Grover, Catfish McDaris, Patrick Simonelli, Julie Demoff Larson, Dr.Timothy Murrae, Misti Rainwater-Lites, Bud Smith, Ron Whitehead, the Juggalos and sweet baby jesus."

And last but certainly not least, we wish to thank our families, our loved ones, and dearest friends. All of our Punk Hostage Press writers currently and those soon to be. And our ever growing literary community. Your support has been paramount and for that we are forever grateful.

~ Iris Berry 2014

INTRODUCTION

I have always thought the creation of a book was like the doctor and the monster waiting for the lightning to strike – when it does and the screams, "It's alive," are heard we know something fantastic has happened. With Punk Hostage Press and Michele McDannold coming together, two admired friends have joined forces to rattle the bones of possibility and something fantastic has happened – *Stealing the Midnight from a Handful of Days*.

Punk Hostage Press has been in my life for a few years now. Its managing partners, Iris Berry and A. Razor have a vision I love. They know "good," have no restraints when reaching for the stars and are not afraid to allow the fantastic to happen. They have created a gateway for a lot of dreams to pass through.

When I first met Michele she was just starting to open up to the world. I remember seeing her poems in one of the "Littles." I commented, she wrote back – I fell in love. I should clarify, I fall in love a lot, but Michele offered something special – a bit of magic, a gentle touch, an uncommon voice. Her poems are elegant in the telling of her innocence. It isn't that she hasn't seen the dark side of the moon, or been touched in undeserving ways. She has. Somehow she has embraced these moments, allowed herself to dream big and has stepped beyond the constraints of a mid-west up-bringing. Her poems come from those deep places, where secrets hide and she writes them with a fearless heart. And yes kid, "You are beautiful."

Michele's *Stealing the Midnight from a Handful of Days*, is the recollection of a young women for whom each moment, breath, event of the day is trapped in memory. She greets sin as common, sorrow as an ally and joy as a mishap.

Punk Hostage Press and Michele McDannold truly have put something fantastic together here. All that's left is for you to love it as much as I do.

Bill Gainer, poet 2014

Whatever
makes you happy
Whatever you want
You're so fucking special
I wish I was
special

But I'm a creep
I'm a weirdo
What the hell am I doing here?
I don't belong here
I don't belong here

~Radiohead

Contents

#1	15
Not Recommended	16
an unnatural and often temporary absence	18
any day now	20
Monkey Bars	21
TOO MUCH	24
So white trash	26
one of the girls	28
Taking it Under Advisement	30
And now she goes by some other name	32
disclosure	34
It's not so bad	35
I am a rock	38
Sign of the Apocalypse	39
i forgot	40
accidentally told you I love you	43
dear fucker	44
sleep, you elusive bitch	46
Spinning Lockstep	47
The Big Gulp	49
Trick	52
animals, every one of us	54
Notes on World Domination	56
I found this poem in a notebook	57
better off dead	58
doorbells, mornings and death	59
empty pages	61
Lost Highway	62
#2	64
So long as you let me take a nap	65
i'm such an asshole	66
A lifetime supply	67
this bored housewife	68
fuck the holidays	69
Joanna	70
Epic	71
Note to the Better Half	72
They Shared an Identity of Interests	73

The Note From Behind the Stamp.................................74
Surprise, You're Dead...75
Relief Status..76
A nice, quiet place 77
lolz 79
Dear Baby Jesus 81
everywhere, someone is dead 86
Dick teasing is out of style 88
don't hold your breath 89
The poets 90
before the resurrection 91
the american dream 92
I should pay my taxes 93
I already paid for my permission 94
I watch this game 96
a tired, diseased yellow 97
today 98
No Malice Intended 99
Aladdin's Lamp 100
The Raw Egg and Grits 101
Café 103
Sloppy Pasta 104
I'm Coming to Get Your Food 105
Cash Business 109
criminally speaking..110
something in the way...111
NOTHING TO LOSE..112
bittersweet 118
Flowers, Mostly Plastic 119
Rubber White and Puckered 121
How to be born-again and feel alright about it........124
hitting my stride 125
#3 128
what else? 129
the facts and details...130
8 horrible ways the universe can destroy us..........132
find a way...134
Cemetery Poem...135

10

To Letting Go

#1

that maybe

if i just stand up

i can make a decision

that takes me

far, far away

from here

and where i've been

maybe

i already did

because sometimes

i swear

this is

all a dream

and in this dream

there is a fantasy

that is real

somewhere else

some other time

when we are

not just stealing

the midnight

from a handful

of days…

Not Recommended

this poetry is not recommended

for the young or bright-eyed

not recommended

for those weak in the stomach

or head

i might use the words

nigger

fag

or retarded

and will definitely use the word

cunt

this poetry is not recommended

for the high-brow

sissified

punk bitches

who would turn a phrase

just to make you feel stupid

poetry is not recommended (period)

if you want to bury your head in the sand

and pretend the world is dying under corruption

we have a voice

this poetry is not recommended

for twitter or myface

you cannot like it

or share it in less than 140 characters

this poetry is not recommended

for NBC

definitely not the Disney channel

we've got balls in our face

and dirt in our shoes

hot shit

red blood

cum stains on the inside pocket

there's a line in the sand that says go fuck yourself

anyone can do this

with enough guts and blaze

to set your ass on fire

an unnatural and often temporary absence

27 messages in the last hour

and i wonder if you could find me

in mexico

i wonder

how helpful it is

to have an epiphany

in your psychiatrist's office--

you are clearly insane

and your perspective

has been warped

for months now

right place, right time?

she asked me if this was

the same outfit

she wore last week

(how embarrassing)

i didn't tell her

i paid more attention to the line

of her bra

and imagined her naked

her soft curls

and

no, i didn't mention

or remember what she wore

"no matter what--

you have to be able

to like yourself,"

she says.

maybe canada,

i think.

they seem awfully pale

up there,

like me.

the phone rings.

time is up.

see you next week.

any day now

staring out
the psychiatrist's window
i see the wind
fucking with a tree
and a smokestack
shaped like a penis
a red, red sports car
the license plates say
MOROW2
i swear

what's green is green
the rest just looks
angry about it
spring is still
fighting its way.

Monkey Bars

Isn't it
just a bit
usual these days
to be talking
shit, fuck?
I was reading this novel
by this great guy
'so and so',
it was only
a few years back,
and it actually said
shit fuck,
shit fuck.
Then later on
when I was reading
some other stuff–
poetry and the like,
well,
I had really
noticed
lots of cunts
for some reason
I've never really
cared for that word,

and don't use it myself,
but back to shit fuck
it's losing power these days
it used to turn heads
even my mother
doesn't flinch anymore
when I let it slip
...fucking shit.

It started for me
on the playground,
a game with Tracey,
the toughest girl in town
who I wanted to be
and Jeff,
the dirtiest boy
in town
who I wanted.
Even in Grade 3,
man, don't tell me
we're not born with it.
so I learned all my
shit fuck
bastard, piss
on the monkey bars
but I never really

perfected it

until the year I worked

in that slaughterhouse.

I was nineteen and desperate.

everyone there was desperate,

shit fuck, became—

"I ain't takin'

no fuckin' shit

piss off, bitch

suck my dick."

It became

an art form

and second nature.

I know at times

you gotta keep it in check

and I do try

to tone it down

but damnit,

it's sewn deep

and when people keep talking

shit fuck, shit fuck,

sometimes,

I hate to hear others say it

sounds cheap,

`cause baby,

it comes at a price.

TOO MUCH

it was the adrenaline

it was the booze

it was nothing

it was everything

it's on the same page

as one sentence, only.

This is too much for me.

It's not leaving my room today

not answering the phone

or returning messages

this is just

the mind-fuck

i've been waiting for

in moments of

I.

don't.

care. about the consequences

it's live the dream

love so much

it hurts

like a bad country song

whatever it was or is

it should be worthy

of a sweet

but salty,

jack & diet coke.

So white trash

i'm doing my best
to ignore the kids
but they are not cooperating
there is no peace
no quiet
there are only
moments of reprieve
when I can sink into the word
fall into a radiohead song
or two
or three
four or five
on loop

i'm a nervous mess
you are out of reach
and need more and more
to fill this new void

so I have
Jack Daniel's,
cigarettes,
coffee,
weed,

writing, writing, writing

the love letters

that will remain

unsent

the confessions

will stay locked up

hiding in the bathroom

sucking down a one-hitter

one of the girls

this one time
i stole the shoelace
of the girl
you were
fucking
down there
in your basement room

removed carefully
from one shoe only
ankle-high granny boots

and when it burnt
at midnight
it smelled of real leather
and lessons
i will
never learn

she was gone
the next week
with the others;

punk girls

pretty girls

nasty girls

reduced to receipts

and the occasional photo

maybe a ticket stub

a one-line tribute

in a poem,

penned late night

at Denny's

which will be remembered

long after

the curve of her ass or

the softness of her...

it is the sum of parts

you forget

crouched down

on the living room floor

surrounded by a circle of salt

the fire in my hand

and fevered head

i have nothing left to give

that you haven't already taken

and mixed in with the rest.

Taking it Under Advisement

he's given me
a lot of good advice
he said,
"kid, tell 'em the stories
and they'll love you for it,
keep it short.
Forget the nonsense.
You gotta get in there,
and out quick
but say something meaningful."

I take it under advisement.
I know he's right- it feels right
and I've got mad respect for the man
but it was those three easy words
that sank the hardest, had the longest bite
"you're beautiful, kid."

it's my nature
to not believe it
but I can't argue
with those confident eyes

he sees me standing there;

not skinny

not plucked

or powdered

or whatever the magazine idea

of a woman

is supposed to be

instead

he sees

I've been hurt,

he sees

I've been healed.

I'm up for the game

and out of regret.

I believe

in the transformative power

of words…

And now she goes by some other name

trina was
the skinniest girl
i had ever seen
hip bones
sticking out
pale,
yellowish skin
and terrible hair
but she had a kindness
and mystical way about her
that was captivating

for a while
she was wiccan
a couple times
a Buddhist
and always
with the tarot cards

she took me to my first
rocky horror picture show
we formed a coven
the boys brought flowers
mowed the lawn

wrote poems,
sketches,
long into the night
acid trips in the park
and no need
for explanations

the worst and most harmful
was her multiple personality disorder
i never really did buy it

it didn't really matter though
after the third abortion
when she told me,
"i went into the bathroom
when he was done.
took that condom out of the trash
and shoved it up there."

one could fairly say
her mind broke then
in some abortion clinic
out west
where he held her hand
watching the light fade
right out of her.

disclosure

doesn't it just

suck shit

that I am not cool.

I am not the idea

of your black death love song

breathing demon blood in vain

but we don't sell happy juice here, either

got out of that business long ago,

I do believe in magic

and since I can find peace in that joy;

I think I'll be alright.

It's not so bad

I see her sitting
on the back steps
trying to hold her head up
with one hand,
a cigarette
with the other

not a shower
or even a sink wash
it's been over 90 degrees
for a week
there's no electricity
no plumbing
hell, the floors are ripped out

a phone call
to the slum lord
and he says,
"oh yeah, I can fix that,"
but he never does…

the extension cord
hangs above her head
as she fingers the key

to the shed

in the back lot

where they store trash

that they pretend

is not trash;

bicycle pieces,

stained mattresses

broken furniture

and on the side

that sits in the shade

a cage

with three bunny rabbits

she hands me a twenty

for the electrical cord hook-up

she says,

on Sundays

the landlord

smells like fried bologna

but it's not so bad

she's had to do worse

to keep a roof

over her head

on a Monday

she let the rabbitts loose

but they kept coming back

to sit in the cage
with the door open wide

and I thought
it might make her sad
and I thought
it might drive her insane
suspended as she was
in a nightmare fairy tale
because I would,
I would find the sharpest knife
and release them all
for good

but she just sat there
continued to sit there
day after
shitty day
smiling
as if waiting
for a picture
to snap,
and the world
to go black…

I am a rock

of sea
of applesauce
of breath in the morning cold

I am a rock
broken and chipped
and weighed down to the bottom

Sign of the Apocalypse

He has pockets

and pockets

and pockets

suspiciously empty in the morning

and full at night

i'm pretending not to notice

the halo

that

in this light

is a bright neon blue

flashing

if you get close enough

(still pretending)

it says

open

Open

OPEN

goddammit

that's what I thought

i forgot

i forgot
how my phone works
i forgot
how to drive
how to go right on red
i forgot
to pick him up on time
i forgot
to take a shower
to wash my clothes
to stand,
walk,
be

i forgot my arm
in the other room
where it cooks,
cleans
and directs traffic
i forgot
to keep moving
in a straight line

basically

i just completely forgot
how to pretend
this is enough

i forgot
to hear the songs
to touch you
one last time
i just fucking forgot

i forgot
that comfort
can kill me
that contentment
will lock me up
and lose the key

i forgot
about grey skies
and cold rain,
puddles with nothing in them
but yesterdays.
goddamn it
how could i forget?

but i remember

i remember now

how to cry

i remember

all too well

this empty feeling

it's just that...

i forgot

how to live with it.

accidentally told you I love you

today i'm paddling back
to my lonely island
of, it's not that heavy
but the boat is sinking, fucker
oh, the boat is sinking

dear fucker

maybe it's okay
just this once…

we live
with the choices
we make shadows
in this fairytale
we're selling,
and walking a line
that is clearly
past the line
believing
it's better
to pretend
not to notice

I'll tell you a secret
(no, i won't)

long gone
are the days
of low tides
and certain outcomes

the room

is a garage-filled cave

freezing

except for

the blue

blue

blue

when i reach for you

i reach

dreams

that live

in the breaking light

i have nothing

to lose

but this…

the sound--

a loop

of fingers

softly playing

this love song

I have lost

everything else

sleep, you elusive bitch

my head is splitting
like dying
like murder
i can't decide which
and so maybe we should
go off in separate rooms
where there are no windows
and the temperature
is 10 degrees below
comfortable.

Spinning Lockstep

these streets

are transient

they ask

when will jesus

take your bitch away

they serve

to sup exploding lights

flying papers

of naked lady delights

day is night

is night is day

the autos just u-turn splash

but the soulless wear tags

professing a devotion to origin

st. louis,

missouri

houston, texas

simply australia

return trip here or there

'cause anywhere isn't nowhere

after you've lived here

come rain or come shine

vegas is the vampire baby

worshiped not nursed

boned not begged

there is no virgin sacrificial blood

this is a hard-core fuck fest

you are worth one dollar

or a thousand or less

cents all translate into minutes

minutes of low-grade air

passing through the valley

just like the tumbleweed

spinning lockstep

over and over yourself

The Big Gulp

About living in vegas...
for the first three weeks,
we lived in a week to week
rental
it was-how shall I say,
questionable.

if you hear screaming,
do not come running.
happen to have a phone
call 911.
'course,
rooms don't come equipped
good luck finding a pay phone
with receiver still attached.

there was a pool though
there is not a hotel/motel/condo/shack
rental of any kind
in vegas that does not have a pool.
I think it's the law.
and, yes.
it had water.

and it was clean.

during the morning hours

when the bulk of the undesirables

were sleeping it off

or still kickin' it, but so fucked

they couldn't be of any real harm

I went swimming

it was bliss.

I don't care what anyone says

about dry heat

115 degrees

is 115 degrees

you sweat your ass off

it just evaporates so fast

it doesn't have time to collect

thank god for 7-11 and the big gulp

if it wasn't for the pool

7-11 and their big gulp,

99 cent shrimp cocktails

down on Freemont street...

free spaghetti dinners

from that trashy casino

with the penny slots,

I never would have made it

those first three weeks.

I never would have hocked
everything I owned to stay on.

Trick

We were loaded...
skimmin' down Morton Ave.
at 4 a.m.,
searching for the end of the fog
where the neon light calls
Takhomasak

you had a counter seat,
cup o' Joe,
the crumbled-up bag at your feet.
laughin' through your story
drop of coffee in your `stache.

"... so he pulls up and says
he's got a bag of canned food for a date.
Ain't that shit funny?
Check it out! I ain't kiddin'."

Juicy brown spit flying on pocket amusement.
(Flo caught it on her uniform sleeve, mortified)

A split-second, maybe a full-tick–
a moment between those two
like the liquid in the torpedo shaped plug in lights

blob o blob, floating, suspended.
Realization squirming up uncomfortable mechanisms
of fate blown anguish.

I wasn't sure who to feel sorry for.

animals, every one of us

there was a lady found in dumpsters
all over town
spread by eight pieces of body parts
all but her head.
it's at this point
i wonder if i might be
in over my neck

in the small towns
we keep our crime quiet
handle it ourselves
or completely ignore it
to the detriment of generation
after generation

wife beating
child molesting
occasional theft
or vandalism, drugs
nobody on the outside needs to know
unless of course
someone breaks out
moves on
then it usually goes

one extreme or the other

a victim- like that lady

or a victimizer...

animals, every one of us.

Notes on World Domination

(relevant is a safe word)

start with the death penalty

shoot-outs

marketing from the Nazis

given over to indoctrination

American Psycho

is cute

but cheesy

and does it better as

Batman

the streets are not the same

I know

the smell of sweat is

everywhere

too much of anything

makes it mean nothing

and can sometimes kill you.

There will never be another underground…

I found this poem in a notebook

(probably a manic fit)

find them a job with the chinese people!
I'm 3 a.m. on any bus outta here
taking my own advice dispensed,
ruffled and fluffed,
a little marked up
if she can take it
I can too
chain-smoking, poetry grenades,
BART rides
kentucky tea
crying
Crying
LAUGHING my ass off
the problems I have now are the
best problems I have ever had
i'm not even 40 yet.

better off dead

maybe I'd be better off dead
than sucking off these words
than percolating the hours away
with a slow-leak to your heart's last drop
maybe I'd be better off dead
than picking at my scabs
than erasing all the jobs I've done
with this broken-ass stub of a pencil
or maybe I'd be better off
deadly
cleaning my teeth with the shards of this thing
with a nice fat roll to my tummy
satisfied
and full
one last time, baby
hiccup

doorbells, mornings and death

or (If you are Cunt)

listen

when you start writing from the brain

chuck it out the door

feed the cats with it

call it meow meow chow

whatever

you've got to be heart, shit or balls

if you're cunt

you better know how to translate

and yes, they'll tell you to stop

and yes, they'll have all kinds of reasons and critiques and

blowhard bullshit

you might even believe for awhile

it will throw you off

maybe you'll take on an old fat fuckin mentor

start writing poems about doorbells, mornings

and death that does not

matter

and maybe everyone pulls a few chains now and then

and maybe everyone has a critic in their heart

and maybe not.

you could or could not say

'and' so much

it wouldn't matter

style has nothing to do with depth

and

if you shovel the shit long enough

you might forget what was under there

you might forget where you were going

you might forget how you were getting there

one day you'll remember

you wanted to go

you'll remember

earth doesn't taste like

dust

heat doesn't feel like

pain

and passion--

doesn't need to be developed.

empty pages

here is the paper

that taught me things

she has ability

she has potential

and an ink that comes to my skin

it fades

like the night

I like to see it coming on the morning

slow

with a tired and wrung-out feeling

it gives way to a new tension

this is the unknown

and I can write this

any way

I want

Lost Highway

this is the straight to hell version
your mother warned you about
an addiction
that you will serve
right up to the bitter end
when things have gone awry
many, many miles back

the top left open
the controls unmanned
one hour
in a roadside motel
at noon

there was a secret compartment
in the floor
off to the corner
where the carpet
was clearly cut

the place is clean
i'll give it that

the man at check-out
hands me a goofy smile
with a comment card
"everything okay?"
he asks
in his broken english

pausing too long
a moment here
could be disastrous
"yes, just fine."

i am on the lost highway
no cell reception
no rest stops
no one asking the wrong questions
and only one
thought --
Linger.

#2

it was always there

right between the lines

subtle

sometimes, not so subtle

and if anyone ever saw it

i never knew

it's a hopeful sort of fear

standing on the platform

tracks, close

vibrating with approach

static electricity

there are many people here

but no one sees

So long as you let me take a nap

i'll stay up with you
push the boundaries
of whatever...
anything
I can't help it
this is realizing
where and who
you're supposed to be
at 6 a.m.
last stop, middle of nowhere
if you can resist
let me know how you did it
I have people and things waiting on me
and they may never come to realization
and I just might not care anyway
if you tell me it's alright
I will
believe

i'm such an asshole

not in the kitchen

not on my way

out the door

not upon waking

goddammit

will i think of you

i will not write

any more

sickening

gay rainbowing

it up

poems.

only assholes

do that

A lifetime supply--

of gobstoppers

children with sticky feet

and no arms to cradle

your pumpkin head

you might be the first

in a long line of

rednecks

it's crystal meth

over sunday dinner

it's no longer barefoot

and pregnant

it's the latest 100 dollar plus

tennis shoe fad

selling your food stamps

for a purse dog

and a flat screen

it's a lifetime of fucking

and fighting

with nothing in between

but a protection order

this bored housewife

plots death by poison on odd days
mornings only
when the kids are gone
and the crock pot's set to high

cuts the hair from your head during the full moon
binds it with duct tape to a piece of ham
while the street is dark
and the dirt is warm

handles
rather than controls
the desire for witch-inspired zombie sex

this bored housewife
has a recipe book
that's time-locked
with a tequila switch
she's just waiting
waiting, waiting
til she can't anymore

fuck the holidays

something's burning
the house down
someone's throwing everything
out on the lawn

granny pissed the couch
and the other grandmother
had to go dry out
it's so mundane
who would bother
making this shit up

smells like
christmas
pledge furniture polish
and childhood disaster

Joanna

she takes ass in the face during the week
in minivans parked on dark corners
on a Tuesday night
1:43 a.m. to be exact

none to be the wiser
'cept she had phoned her friend
to say she'd taken
black nipple in her mouth

her husband later responds
oh shit
when told of the news
on the daily cell phone call

pulls his semi-truck over
to the side of the road
for a quick pull -
to find himself crying over his diseased cock
in his hand

This is how people with no skills get along in life,
Joanna, tells me.

Epic

my epic poem is a list of groceries
sorted by things I can buy
generic and not
the hero is a box of Pop-Tarts
because let's face it
nobody else can get the filling right

next to my bed
is the stepford wives
ear plugs
and a basket of lubes, lotions
and creams
for not having sex
for not looking younger
for not healing
the hole in my head

Note to the Better Half

I miss the smell of mass deviation

of latino santa sweat

and artie's chronic n gun oil

I miss the pulse of drunk transit at 3 a.m.

black hookers in white wigs

and white pimps in purple satin

I miss the homeless junkies

and the rest stop houses

with sound systems

too big to fit

and fuckers too drunk to shoot, not fuck

I miss the rain that flooded my car

the stink that followed

and the body parts that washed up

yes, I miss being in love

on the run

and even pawning my only diamond

someday soon

there'll be a note void of tears

and dinners in the icebox

that freeze a lot better than I do.

They Shared an Identity of Interests

I was given a line once

from a poem

I was told to take it into life

make it alive

make it a home

give it a new name

so there were sidewalks

running without shoes

cold on your feet

like an icebox empty of love

there was a tricycle

spinning wheels

faster than Speed Racer

take me on the back

I'll stand

and hold on

forever

The Note From Behind the Stamp

if I am not in love

what can I tell you

there is not much left

worth

the ink

Surprise, You're Dead

I'm scared of my neighbor's eyes,

my landlord's tentacles.

Wonder if this small-town life

is worth the low crime rate,

the faint smell of home

and knowing

all the streets

not by name

but a feel

rooted in twenty years ago.

Taking the back road along the cemetery

there's a utility pole

with the words

"Fuck Life"

spray-painted

up the side.

It seems like the right place to be

and I am envious.

Relief Status

"There's a holocaust in my driveway,"
she tells me
a puddle of black
crude oil, that is
Texas Tea.

Ask me a thousand ways, lady
the lies are the same ...
Relief Status;
IN PROCESS,
PENDING,
UNKNOWN.

I already know
she's fucked from here to
election day
at the very least.

A nice, quiet place

we don't have prostitutes,
crackheads
or faggots
hangin around the streets,
spreading their disease.

no niggers 'cept that one side of town.
when they shoot at each other -
we don't care.

we have more fast food places
than proper dining.
the walmart on the edge of town
is the place to be.

we like deep-fried, double-dipped
ignorance
served with a side of hypocrisy.

it's a nice, quiet place to live.
the criminals are advertised
in the newspaper and
on channel 2.

the real thieves

(of dignity, of justice)

yes, those cunts--

they walk in plain sight.

at least they have the "decency"

to put their dogshit in a bag,

raise their flag high

and lock their guns up

at night.

god bless us,

every one.

lolz

it's not my fault
i was born into
a redneck town
that hates niggers
and hides the innocence
of children
under a riverbed

poor, in a trailer
at a relative's
passed around
from one abuse
to the next

but i am not your victim
sorry, diet fads
sorry, dr phil
sorry, Oprah

when you learn certain things
too early
it fucks your head

the funniest thing i ever heard

at a poetry reading
was a rape poem

i expect neither of us
needs to apologize

Dear Baby Jesus

Thank you for the best childhood ever

for the nicely manicured lawns

dutifully tended to every Sunday

after church

for the sun tea baking on the porch

and the strawberries in the patch

Thank you, baby jesus

for the community free of minorities

and forward thinking

for the streets free of gang violence

for the jehovah's witness even

and the evangelists

thank you for putting the shame on

all those unwed and/or single mothers

those people with the weak-minded mental illnesses

and the ghastly homosexuals

in general, just thank you so much

for putting a clamp down

on all the SEX stuff

I didn't know what my period was

until I got it one day in gym

that kinda sucked

but thank you

and maybe while you were hiding

all the dildos and other adult fun

you could have taught the old people

not to stick their fingers and whatnot

in the young people

that would have been nice

but oh well

maybe that's why Billy Bob's uncle

is also his dad

I never met anyone conceived from incest before

COOL

thank you, baby jesus

I know. I know

some people want to give all the credit to Satan

Lucifer

the Devil

whatever

he's busy with wars

tsunamis

and shit

he wants the glory of all those big fatality numbers

you... you are oh so patient

killing them softly and gently

with shitty lives

contrived of stifling rules...

call it morality!

Shame, shame

the bent and twisted

call it love

BABY JESUS

I want you to have all the credit

saving us all from the fires of Hell

I can pray to you for forgiveness

I can pray to you for the Friday night football game

we can all join hands and pray pray pray

then sing the star spangled banner

oh, thank you, baby jesus

for making me an American

thank you for making us better

than every other nation in the world

so what if we drop the ball

in our schools

turn our backs

on mother nature

and would turn out

anyone or anything

in the best interest

of the almighty dollar

we are responsible for FACEBOOK

Honey Boo Boo

and taco shells made out of Doritos!

this is all thanks to you, baby jesus

but, wait...

I have more rights to my guns

than my own body!!

sweet baby jesus

thank you

oh, thank you

for Women that know their place

in dresses

in kitchens

in the delivery room

children, children, children

let's have more babies, baby jesus!

Every last one of them, precious

until they learn to breathe

in the polluted

but free as all fuck

liberty-laced air

everywhere, someone is dead

where are the living?
not down the street on the main stretch
packed into cars, stalling in traffic at noon
baked in the heat, counting
gallons of gas
burning more
and
more dollar signs evaporating
with the carbon
monoxide and food
money
gone, no
more money left
for medicine or the utility bill

forget school
forget resumes
nothing's left for you

the gap is ever widening

the forecast said 97
and mr. news reporter reports--

if you're not going over 45 mph

keep the windows down

you're moving too slow.

Dick teasing is out of style

let's count backward from one thousand

and make pretty art slobber together

bedazzled eyebags

I cannot see

but no one else can either

let's smoke pot now

the day of the dead is near

don't hold your breath

for strange

that waits in line

they have the urgent on

the dead-eye

of target/missile games

and still they

miss everything

worth

not missing

The poets

They are too loud
yammering and bullshitting
poeticizing
but when they are gone
when it is quiet
I am empty

before the resurrection

I quit my job on good friday
I can't help it
that my sense of humor is kinda whack
and I believe that

shutting doors
is better than jumping out windows

the american dream

is a pair of pouty lips
stuffed in six inches of heel
I have excuses for flab that range from
silly to you can't dispute the benefits
of breast feeding
there's a shade of lipstick for that
and matching nail color
I figure I should quit smoking first
nicotine stains on fingers and teeth
but I will not lie
I love it
and do what I want
damn the consequences
that-- is the american dream

I should pay my taxes

contribute to society
start a war
in my neighborhood
of lawn clippings
and garden gnomes
I wave at the neighbor
and he hates me right back

this quiet loathing
of property lines
and sagging trees
could put us both down

I already paid for my permission

at the food bank
it was expired cans of
fruit salad
and
stewed tomatoes

at the family resource center
there's a box in the back
where they keep the self-respect

pulling out my link card
at the grocery, in the checkout line
the lady behind me
wears a beautiful scarf
and a cute handbag
a cart full of fresh fruits and veggies
she's staring at my cheap,
overly processed boxes of food
and chunks of red meat,
my kid with his ipod ...
she shakes her head.

at the social security office
their 500 question survey

about my schedule, my habits
and my inability to _____

it's the same everywhere
what you lack in money
you pay in your humanity

I jump up on the table in the junior high cafeteria
singing Harper Valley PTA
nobody gets it
or laughs

i paid my dues
learned my lessons--

don't throw out those dented cans
the overzealous coupon purchases
don't throw anything away
i'm going to need it
i'm going to need all the buffer I can get
lest they take my overburdened soul
and recycle it for brownie points

I watch this game

from over here in my
little sandbox
it's a vantage point
I've come both to rely on
and suffer from
carefully construed moat
in case the barricade fails
it's high,
so I can barely climb
my rickety shit
to spy on this damn circus marauder
he is that one and she are all
the same
when I look close enough
their laughing looks like me too,
it's just plain rude

a tired, diseased yellow

lost on the internet,
sifting through faces
i'm supposed to know--
the only witnesses to my lonely
and desperate choices.

i'm tired,
all too absorbed in the past.
this is an empty motel room,
reserved,
not paid for.

today

i only mean what i say
when i keep it to myself
it might be back alley logic
but it keeps my conscience clear

today it's raining
my heart pounds louder
than the drops hitting the roof tins
the sound of love, dropped
just shy of realization

i think of how easy it is
to get by
the cold night is near
you slip a bottle in my hand
and look at me like you're seeing yesterday

there is no tomorrow
and this, i keep
to myself

No Malice Intended

I fall, more often than not
just to the left of your shade
an empty bottle of spray
a used sandwich wrapper
the bottle cap
I'm below you, I know
from my vantage point, I see
though there are days I pretend
your swift kicks are
like the children, you are playing
as they do make a game of it

Aladdin's Lamp

Shouldn't have moments of realization in motel rooms
fake cups wrapped in plastic that they are
half-full, the cup ripped open
to serve my butt and ash turned to muck

Every crook you ever knew hangs on these walls
pictures sold from black and white catalogue
half-wit, cutthroat competition
to sell their ass like the whore they are

and what have I done
lamplight burning 24/7
why bother with the clothes either
stacks on desks and tables of pizza boxes
not of novels or poems or papers

and the leaky window air conditioner says
buzz
buzz
buzz

The Raw Egg and Grits

the racial profiling in the kitchen is out of control

this man's voice transposes

the chords of Hunter S. Thompson

It's the violin's strings wiggling

slurs

I feel I've had too much

sugar

or otherwise

inactive ingredients

he is not wise

I suspect he thinks he is

talking loud enough to take pride

in absurdity

if you listen carefully

in the café

you can hear the

catfish growing

you can hear the

1963 Ford

how it was

a Maroon that resembled

the letting go of a youth

you hear a groomed wisdom

sold over stories

well, some are true

and others are imagined so

something about keeping his coat shiny in Texas

and how he says Aaaa`

knows everything

about something

talks from a napkin

like the blood meeting air comes out blue

the words dribble out the mouth, tastes of poetry

shades that collide and fight for room

he says

if the cook is Mexicano

he might understand the raw egg

even better

the black man

can't go wrong on the grits

Café

We pick up from the streets, words
and skin stretched
thin over
mother's lips.
Dumpster love along the spillway, free;
sunshine through the way. She
dances to the jukebox,
a knife in back of cowboy lust
to celebrate the waitress.

Open sign askew a door
of rust and nails of regret
scratchandspitandspew
coffee dust.

Sloppy Pasta

what if I said I didn't want to FUCK YOU
not in yr agoraphobic lexicon pasty ego-trip
sweat pant adjective sideshow
what if I, then
said I loved most of your verbs but none of your nouns
how they looked de
pressed, sounded evermore like
doing the noodle
and it just won't stick, baby.
it just won't stick.

I'm Coming To Get Your Food

I'm thinking of moving
perhaps I will go
where there is a good
Food Pantry

Being poor is a matter
of shifting
shifting things around
until things get better

Las Vegas, Nevada
Population 478,434
does not have
a desirable Food Bank

Back in '95
I open'd up a package
of dry blueberry muffin mix
with much excitement
I dumped 'er in the bowl
and cracked
my eggs right in

(those were some of my last

few cents — those eggs.

No eggs at the Food Pantry
and groceries don't come cheap
in the land of endless buffets)

I stirred like I hadn't eaten in days
because *I hadn't eaten in days*

dipped
my fingers into the batter
for a taste test
just before she reached
my tongue, mouth agape
my eyes spotted the tiny mealworms
swimming
around the mixing bowl

DAMN!

My Finger
The Bowl
my finger, the bowl

eyes darting back and forth
Should I?

God, I am SO hungry.

protein,

right?

How many times had I heard that

accidentally swallowed a bug

— didn't kill me.

I'm still alive.

Still standing here.

But, for how friggin' long…

FUCK!

[splat]

(blueberry-worm wall food)

Note To Self:

thank Food Pantry for Pine-Sol—

quite handy in Dining Room

Yes, the smaller towns

though, not too small

they get the better stuff

fresh stuff

They get all society

and competitive

about their Food Banks

like

Jacksonville, IL

Population 18,940

You can even get fresh Bakery goods
on certain days.

It's the bomb.

Cash Business

Don't send it

the waxing poetic

is a stick fuck

if I imagined in colors it would be

black and blackblue

if it had feelers, velvet

and punk renditions of showtunes

it's true that I paint it up to avoid reality

and it's ugly like that

I suppose that's the point

in the end

everyone pays for truth

criminally speaking

I'm considering one of those robberies

where they drive a truck through a

convenience store

and take off with an ATM

but i'm too lazy, old and broken for this

a criminal by definition

cheating welfare

driving without insurance

stupid poor shit like that

I don't have the balls for serious drug abuse,

highway robbery

or even jaywalking

my crime is denial and safety

as I type these words

i'm already fingering the delete key

something in the way

so many w/ great hair

and bad eyesight

if the moon

were a spork

well, ya know

even the cat is sick of it

there is nothing

but to sleep

to grind

to slide forward

to be

a lightning bug

smacked to the windshield

glowing bright

for one more

moment

Nothing to Lose (or Freedom)

i need to be

that guy ...

the next one in line

as the door closes,

the last one picked,

the "we just sold out"

of every kind of whatever

you're looking for,

the flat tire,

the flat busted...

left for dead,

fucked over six ways

to Sunday,

guy.

that guy whose lover

stole a pigeon heart

and took a big dump

on his head.

fuckery, so insane

so very needless...

all reason, if there ever

was any--

is totally obliterated.

i

want to be that guy

"that kind of pissed that leads not to revenge

but to a reckoning"

people will shed a lone tear

sniffle

and shake their head a lot

i will keep on gathering great poems

sharing the news about great poets

new ones

old ones

killer ones

fucky ones

we'll call it

the "didn't make it to twitter

because it had too much

character" book

i want to drive down the great river road

i want a reading

right now!

in bars

bookstores

and bowling alleys

i want to read/scream

at bikers and rednecks

housewives and whores

i hope they throw stuff

and spit on me

chase me out to the car

yelling

"we don't like your kind

'round here"

but they will secretly

worship me

and my freedom

and my hoard of poets

from the suburbs

the city

the farm

they're multiplying like gremlins

one dash of sit and spin

and they're out ruining christmas

i want them all

(not to make them famous)

to make them infamous

to spread their disease

of think

of cut out the bullshit

and get to the point

i want America

in her glazed over Red Bull eyes

to really

really

wake the fuck up

this is no time to let it ride

the great depression

is your brain on ice

your investment in image

the "i'm okay- you're okay" is a dead hippie lie

the 1% is selling everything

is selling you, me..

McDonald's and Twilight books

medication via

TV ads

the party is over

the beatniks are dead or dying

the outlaws are a joke

the wild west is tamed, my friends

rail against that which seeks to defeat you

every day

every hour

RIGHT NOW

get in your car

go

don't kill the first thing that gets in your way

kill em all

kill em all

kill em all,

motherfuckers.

they call us the X generation

with nothing to lose

but our Nirvana CDs

and Fight Club on DVD

didn't you get the memo?

the *they* have

co-opted your identity for mass marketing

you can now buy

the special edition director's cut t-shirt snuggie toothpick rim job

with decal

get the fuck

OUT

out of your house

and stick a fist up their ass for doing this

don't buy the hype

use it against them

like those goddamn

nothing to lose

asshole poets

that you love

bittersweet

you're walking barefoot on the last day

of your forever summer

too damn cold

to feel the asphalt melt into

the wind

smiling

the way you smile

before the frigid air

takes the something

that's been in your skin for so long

Flowers, Mostly Plastic

in the back yard
I had a big mound of sand
two times, maybe three, my height
supposing to play in
sometimes I even did

building castles, forts and things
more often than not, I sat on the edge of the yard
where there was a plot of concrete
planned once for a basketball court, I think
there I would sit
on the cool cement among the abandoned,
rusting metal toy cars
and watch

I was watching the wind blow
and the shadow fall
I was watching every tiny distracting sense
of the moment
as it passed
in the graveyard next door

I watched the people come, though not often
I watched the flowers, mostly plastic

I watched them fall and tumble
I watched them scoot, almost play
one day here, another there
among the gravestones
I watched the seasons change
the leaves on the trees to the ground
and the man working
I would hide then, behind the shed
watching in secret

how do they care for their dead?
(I did not think of that then)

Rubber White and Puckered

I dreamt of living in a rubber room

(my head wrapped around a train)

the whistle

it doesn't sound like a whistle

not like the old western movies

when I say old

(I mean dead, they seem dead)

that black and white trapped in a box

must be bones

it is similar to the pale mornings

when I visit the mausoleum

in the back where the tiles pull out

no one comes here anymore

not to see the picture behind glass that was Sampson

that was Julia

they don't notice a dead bird brought in from the rain

No

the tiles are white

all else is ash grey

black

the train sounds

a horn

a horn that won't let up

on and on it goes

as it reaches the end of my mind

the sound fades

end of the track

the last stand of town

the sound of the rails

the rumbling

a vibration

rattling windows

there are no windows here

only rubber

rubber white and puckered

[in the room, we are back in the room]

with buttons

small, round

it looks like a couch

all the way round the room

(you can find death in rooms too)

you can see the door is the outlined shape of a door

sticks out from the rest

it feels like I could run

run into it

and the sound

the sound might go away

How to be born-again and feel alright about it

get too drunk too fast

close your eyes and spin spin spin

where's the weed?

He's laughing in my ear

and i'm hiding from the other room

this is normal, right?

Jesus was a baby and always will be

temporary alcoholism

permanent un-inhibition

water saves the day

hitting my stride

i go for walks
at 5 a.m.
before the morning
is light
where the moon
still has dominion
and all the stray dogs
and stray thoughts
are asleep
under someone's porch
or behind the dumpster
maybe in a field covered with
dying weeds
out of sight
out of mind

the walkway is broken
but calm
and this i can appreciate

it is just me
the wind if there is any
sometimes i see
the man delivering papers

i hear him first
the footsteps
that remind me of
absolutely nothing
i have no fear
the day is blank

the asian woman
is sweeping her
leaves
from the lawn
meticulous care
and possible
obsession
we pretend not to
notice each other
as if i am listening
to music
watching my step
focused on the path
ahead
sidestep a puddle
hold my breath
when i pass the
sewer grate
circle around the

neighborhood

once

twice

three times

then i let my eyes wander to her side of the

street

she looks up

right at that moment

and says simply

good morning -- good exercise

"yes it is"

was all i could

think to say

not missing a beat

one sneakered foot

after another

rounding the corner

as the darkness is

giving way

#3

i'm not going to torture you with this

loving down to the bones

what we have

is impossible

and yet somehow

true

for every person that

came back from the

brink

throw me a

line

before i sink

completely

what else?

we seek

the limits of oblivion

the arms

secrets

and unveiling

we are

to our detriment

laughing

the facts and details

at some point

you'll start to wonder

where i left you

and went with those other men

i start to think

and smoke some more drugs

what is the difference

between

instructions and directions

you won't want to know

his arms worked better than yours

in holding me down

your mouth is the lack of,

i dream–

still…

rinse,

repeat

veer right at the curve

if you have to crash

go to your right

if you have to

this highway leads to

this highway

and nothing else

8 horrible ways the universe can destroy us

and they happened without warning

the fade

the cut and run

the never was what you thought in the first place

the dry, sucking ache of just not right

the disconnect

the gray the gray the gray

it's about

cutting things down

to the quick

something that

happens

without warning

when you think

too much

& hold it in

i apologize in advance

your metaphors

are like

a sandbag

in a desert

today

is the

beginning

of the end

i have already cried enough

find a way

find a way to be invisible

flesh-colored

costume

that blends well

with the starless night

your hand on my mouth

i feel nothing now

goodnight dots

goodnight cursor

blinking

a safe word

with a stranger is

Yes.

goodnight love

deconstruct this poem

in the morning

Cemetery Poem (for my love)

i'm sitting here at the
cemetery
talking to myself
i think i'll probably
be here awhile
be doing this
wondering all along
if it will be enough

this is where i go
when none of it makes sense
just so you know

where it is quiet
my mind quiets
there is some sort of peace
in the finality

i think of papa
his letters
sent home while
out on the river
or out to sea
for months

and months on end
starting the letter, stopping
and beginning again
if only a sentence or two
in between the work
that keeps him away

how he called her
my love
and still she
drank just a little too much
a little too often

all this i learn from old letters
see in yellowed photographs

how she stared off-center
with a sadness around
the eyes
only laughing in the photo
when he's seated next to her
and all those years
since she died
he lived on, puttering
through life

i wonder if he
pretended she was there
for the rest of it
for the baseball games
over the radio
the mornings in the garden
the looking out over
everything
wondering...
what does it matter
anyway

today on duncan avenue
in diamond grove cemetery
it does not matter
i talk to myself
i will lie down
in the earth by myself
search for you
in the next life
and hope
it will be easier

Michele McDannold

Born in Jacksonville, Illinois, Michele McDannold grew up in the nearby village of Meredosia, population never more than 1200. She has lived in west central Illinois most of her life except for one year in Las Vegas and a short stint in Nebraska. Michele started writing poetry in grade school and maintained a connection with writing as an occasional pastime and coping mechanism. It was not until her early thirties that she began pursuing her poetry seriously and seeking publication. Since then, her poetry has been published in a wide range of print and online publications and anthologies.

Having only recently returned to a university to further her education, Michele's writing style is self-taught, developing over time and life experience, aided by her *sick* love for books. Her poetry tends toward the narrative—daily and life observations told in colloquial speech. Her perspective comes from that of a marginalized artist struggling with poverty, mental illness, motherhood and society's expectations of a woman and wife living in a small Midwestern town.

Michele is no new comer. She has been and still is an active participant, making a huge impact in the small press community for a number of years now. She was the Editor-in-Chief at *Red Fez Publications* for over five years, and in her own words, "for about as long as the most awesomest director Leopold McGinnis could stand for it." She is the founder of *The Literary Underground*, a grassroots effort committed to supporting independent artists, promoting diversity in creativity and fostering community in the small press communities. Michele is currently the editor/publisher for *Citizens For Decent Literature Press*, actively working on the *This Is Poetry* project with co-editor Brian W. Fugett of *Zygote in my Coffee* and proud as hell to have published the book of poetry *Random Acts of Terror* by Luis Rivas. In her spare time (haha), she helps Catfish McDaris out over at *Ppigpenn*--a literary arts blogzine, and those folks over at *Blotterature Literary Magazine* pretend to listen to the rambling on occasion.

Michele currently resides in Jacksonville, Illinois with her two teenage children and occasionally her wayward twenty-year old child. She is a full-time student and does a massive amount of hustle to keep the dream alive. Her cat's name is Ghost. He leaves her dead things as *offerings*.

www.michelemcdannold.com

More about Michele McDannold

Michele McDannold does not waste a lot of time with fancy metaphors and pretty literary things. She builds straight to the punch, and she doesn't hit like a girl. This is poetry as it should be. Not covered up and shrouded in riddles. Not poeticizing about flowers and Spring. This is truth. This is a punch straight to the gut.

–Michael Grover, poetry editor of Red Fez Publications

Stealing the Midnight from a Handful of Days is the kind of perfect art that should be read aloud over a Walmart PA system as it begins to burn down.

–Bud Smith, author of Tollbooth

As we plummet south talk to me whisper in my ears words i can't possibly understand sing all night as we speed from las vegas to hollywood do your michele mcdannold stealing the midnight from a handful of days punk hostage press fuck you scream in arabic to telephone poles mowing them down with electric guitar never more than four chords...

–Ron Whitehead, outlaw poet

So much poetry…classic poetry, academic poetry, award winning poetry, small press poetry…is pure shit. I read it and dismiss it and it leaves my brain, thankfully. Michele McDannold's poetry is not shit. It does not leave my brain, thankfully. I am constipated with Michele McDannold's lines and I am very glad. Here's to the ones who are not cool, who don't try to be cool, who just write their fucking truth line by fucking line in syllables that sing to the sky.

–Misti Rainwater-Lites, poet

OTHER PUNK HOSTAGE PRESS BOOKS

FRACTURED (2012) by Danny Baker

BETTER THAN A GUN IN A KNIFE FIGHT (2012)
by A. Razor

THE DAUGHTERS OF BASTARDS (2012) by Iris Berry

DRAWN BLOOD: COLLECTED WORKS FROM
D.B.P.LTD., 1985-1995 (2012) by A. Razor

IMPRESS (2012) by C.V.Auchterlonie

TOMORROW,YVONNE - POETRY & PROSE FOR

SUICIDAL EGOISTS
(2012) by Yvonne De la Vega

BEATEN UP BEATEN DOWN (2012) by A. Razor

MIRACLES OF THE BLOG: A SERIES (2012)
by Carolyn Srygley--Moore

8TH & AGONY (2012) by Rich Ferguson

SMALL CATASTROPHES IN A BIG WORLD (2012) by A. Razor

UNTAMED (2013) by Jack Grisham

MOTH WING TEA (2013) by Dennis Cruz

HALF-CENTURY STATUS (2013) by A. Razor

SHOWGIRL CONFIDENTIAL (2013) by Pleasant Gehman

BLOOD MUSIC (2013) by Frank Reardon

I WILL ALWAYS BE YOUR WHORE/LOVE SONGS for Billy
Corgan (2014) by Alexandra Naughton

A HISTORY OF BROKEN LOVE THINGS (2014) by SB Stokes

YEAH, WELL... (2014) by Joel Landmine

DREAMS GONE MAD WITH HOPE (2014) by S.A. Griffin

CODE BLUE: A LOVE STORY (2014) by Jack Grisham

HOW TO TAKE A BULLET AND OTHER SURVIVAL POEMS (2014) by Hollie Hardy

SCARS (2014) by Nadia Bruce-Rawlings

WHEN I WAS A DYNAMITER (2014) by Lee Quarnstrom

DEAD LIONS (2014) by A.D. Winans

FORTHCOMING BOOKS ON PUNK HOSTAGE PRESS:

THUGNESS IS A VIRTUE (2014) by Hannah Wehr

WHERE THE ROAD LEADS (2015) by Diana Rose

LONGWINDED TALES OF A LOW PLAINS DRIFTER (2015)
by A. Razor

EVERYTHING IS RADIANT BETWEEN THE HATES (2015)
by Rich Ferguson

GOOD GIRLS GO TO HEAVEN, BAD GIRLS GO EVERYWHERE
by Pleasant Gehman (2015)

BOULEVARD OF SPOKEN DREAMS (2015) by Iris Berry

DANGEROUS INTERSECTIONS (2015) by Annette Cruz

DRIVING ALL OF THE HORSES AT ONCE (2015)
by Richard Modiano

DISGRACELAND (2015)
by Iris Berry & Pleasant Gehman

AND THEN THE ACID KICKED IN (2015)
by Carlye Archibeque

BODIES: BRILLIANT SHAPES (2015) by Kate Menzies

BORROWING SUGAR (2015) by Susan Hayden

BASTARD SONS OF ALPHABET CITY (2015) by Jon Hess

THE REDHOOK GIRAFFE & OTHER BROOKLYN TALES (2015)
by James A. Tropeano III

PURO PURISMO (2015) by A. Razor

IN THE SHADOW OF THE HOLLYWOOD SIGN (2015)
by Iris Berry

SIRENS (2015) by Larry Jaffe

www.ingramcontent.com/pod-product-compliance
Lightning Source LLC
Chambersburg PA
CBHW020938090426
42736CB00010B/1178